I0748450

Published by Angelis Publications
ISBN: 978-1-912484-18-8
www.angelispublications.com
© 2019 Angelis Publications
All rights reserved

benvinguda
roimh
Velkomin
grata
Croeso
vitajte
üdvözöljük
Bem
menyambut
vitejte
welkom
Bienvenue
Benvido
widziane
Sveiki
benvenuti
willkommen
bienvenida
malligayang
velkommen
venit
Välkomna
пожаловать
tervetuloa
Сардэчна
welcome
dobrodošli
просимо
mile
Ласкаво
Mừng
ai
velkomen
chào
Добро
sveikt
fáilte
vindo

A Welcome Message To Our Guests

Date / Name / From	Comments

Date / Name / From	Comments

Date / Name / From	Comments

Date / Name / From	Comments

Date / Name / From	Comments

Date / Name / From	Comments

Date / Name / From	Comments

Date / Name / From	Comments

Date / Name / From	Comments

Date / Name / From	Comments

Date / Name / From	Comments

Date / Name / From	Comments

Date / Name / From	Comments

Date / Name / From	Comments

Date / Name / From	Comments

Date / Name / From	Comments

Date / Name / From	Comments

Date / Name / From	Comments

Date / Name / From	Comments

Date / Name / From	Comments

Date / Name / From	Comments

Date / Name / From	Comments

Date / Name / From	Comments

Date / Name / From	Comments

Date / Name / From	Comments

Date / Name / From	Comments

Date / Name / From	Comments

Date / Name / From	Comments

Date / Name / From	Comments

Date / Name / From	Comments

Date / Name / From	Comments

Date / Name / From	Comments

Date / Name / From	Comments

Date / Name / From	Comments

Date / Name / From	Comments

Date / Name / From	Comments

Date / Name / From	Comments

Date / Name / From	Comments

Date / Name / From	Comments

Date / Name / From	Comments

Date / Name / From	Comments

Date / Name / From	Comments

Date / Name / From	Comments

Date / Name / From	Comments

Date / Name / From	Comments

Date / Name / From	Comments

Date / Name / From	Comments

Date / Name / From	Comments

Date / Name / From	Comments

Date / Name / From	Comments

Date / Name / From	Comments

Date / Name / From	Comments

Date / Name / From	Comments

Date / Name / From	Comments

Date / Name / From	Comments

Date / Name / From	Comments

Date / Name / From	Comments

Date / Name / From	Comments

Date / Name / From	Comments

Date / Name / From	Comments

Date / Name / From	Comments

Date / Name / From	Comments

Date / Name / From	Comments

Date / Name / From	Comments

Date / Name / From	Comments

Date / Name / From	Comments

Date / Name / From	Comments

Date / Name / From	Comments

Date / Name / From	Comments

Date / Name / From	Comments

Date / Name / From	Comments

Date / Name / From	Comments

Date / Name / From	Comments

Date / Name / From	Comments

Date / Name / From	Comments

Date / Name / From	Comments

Date / Name / From	Comments

Date / Name / From	Comments

Date / Name / From	Comments

Date / Name / From	Comments

Date / Name / From	Comments

Date / Name / From	Comments

Date / Name / From	Comments

Date / Name / From	Comments

Date / Name / From	Comments

Date / Name / From	Comments

Date / Name / From	Comments

Date / Name / From	Comments

Date / Name / From	Comments

Date / Name / From	Comments

Date / Name / From	Comments

Date / Name / From	Comments

Date / Name / From	Comments

Date / Name / From	Comments

Date / Name / From	Comments

Date / Name / From	Comments

www.ingramcontent.com/pod-product-compliance
Lightning Source LLC
Chambersburg PA
CBHW081126300726
48982CB00005B/861

* 9 7 8 1 9 1 2 4 8 4 1 8 8 *